GUIDE THEM TO JESUS

Experience His Life, Teaching, and Miracles with Your Kids

Shawna Goldstein

Copyright 2021 by Shawna Goldstein
No part of this book may be reproduced in any form or by any means
without written consent from the author.

ISBN : 9798474511900

Unless otherwise noted, all Scripture is
New International Version, copyright 1978, Zondervan Press.

Cover art and graphic design by Kylie Whitman

TABLE OF CONTENTS

Week 1 - The Word Became Flesh
Timeline: The Word, Prophesy, Birth | Memorize: John 3:16-17

Week 2 - Preparing for Ministry
Timeline: Growing, Baptism, Temptation | Memorize: Matthew 4:4

Week 3 - Miracles of Jesus
Timeline: Miracles, Storm, Child | Memorize: John 14:1

Week 4 - Miracles Part 2
Timeline: Roof, 5000 Fed, Walks on Water | Memorize: Matthew 21:21

Week 5 - Parables of Jesus
Timeline: Parables, Lost | Memorize: Luke 19:10

Week 6 - Parables Part 2
Timeline: 4 Soils, Good Samaritan | Memorize: John 15:5, Matthew 22:37-39

Week 7 - Teachings of Jesus
Timeline: Teachings, Sermon on the Mount | Memorize: Matthew 5:9

Week 8 - Teachings Part 2
Timeline: Pray, Harvest | Memorize: Matthew 5:16

Week 9 - Jesus and People
Timeline: Eats with Sinners, Mary and Martha | Memorize: John 13:35

Week 10 - Holy Week
Timeline: Palm Sunday, Feet, Garden | Memorize: John 14:6

Week 11 - Holy Week Part 2
Timeline: Died, Buried, Rose | Memorize: John 11:25-26

Week 12 - Hope for Today
Timeline: Holy Spirit, Ascended, Returning | Memorize: John 16:33, Matthew 28:19-20

Leader Guide

INTRODUCTION

Welcome! Will you pause with me and take a moment to prepare your heart to encounter Jesus the next 12 weeks? You don't have to come alone; you are a disciple who is already making more disciples. So grab your kids and bring them to sit at the feet of Jesus with you. We will explore events from Jesus' life, His interactions with people, His teaching, and His miracles. Together we'll memorize words that He spoke. You will be His student, but my hope is that by the end of this journey, He will be your best friend.

In writing this study, my goal was to meet you in the midst of your busy schedule, bringing the Word to you in small workable chunks that you can share with your children. The good news is if you don't complete any work at home, you're still 100% prepared for group time. Everything you'll need for the moms group discussion will be done together.

As you follow along, you and your kids will encounter the major events and teachings from the life of Jesus. Each week, there is at least one suggested memory verse to learn that was spoken by Jesus Himself. Place these verses in your home where you will see them and review them often (by yourself and with your kids)! Any day that you don't have new material to cover, you can review the timeline and all memory verses that you've learned thus far, perhaps at night with bedtime prayers. (A suggested model for praying with your kids is provided in the Week 1 material.)

The kids' portion of this study is designed for ages 2 and up. Though little ones may not be able to do it all by memory, they will grasp major ideas and will remember more than you think. If you have a child under age 2, or even an infant, I encourage you to still do the reading with them. God promises that His Word will never return void. You never know what seeds you are sowing in their hearts for eternity. Extension reading is provided for grade school children, and for that I suggest reading in an NIrV Bible, which is designed for young readers. If you don't own this or other suggested versions, you can look them up on biblegateway.com. For teenagers, consider inviting them into the "Just for Mom" portion in addition to the study for kids!

Now, imagine you're taking your children's hands and leading them to the shade of a tree where Jesus is teaching. Curl up on a blanket on the grass and get ready to learn with your kids at the feet of Jesus.

-Shawna

LIFE OF JESUS TIMELINE

(Events are ordered for ease of learning and may not be chronological.)

The Word, Prophesy, Birth, Growing,
Baptism, Temptation,
MIRACLES: Storm, Child, Roof,
5000 Fed, Walks on Water,
PARABLES: Lost, 4 Soils, Good Samaritan,
TEACHINGS: Sermon on the Mount,
Pray, Harvest,
Eats with Sinners, Mary and Martha,
Palm Sunday, Feet, Garden, Died,
Buried, Rose, Holy Spirit, Ascended,
Returning

Week 1:
The Word Became Flesh

MOMS GROUP DISCUSSION

Read Genesis 1:1-2 and John 1:1-5.

At the creation of the world, what three "parts" of God are present?

Read John 1:14-18.

What happened to the "Word"?

How does this passage show that Jesus is eternal?

How does this passage show that Jesus is God?

God knew all along that the Word would one day become flesh (Jesus, fully God and fully man) to take away the sins of the world. Because this was the plan from the start, and God exists outside of time and space (meaning He knows what will happen in the future), God was able to reveal truths about Jesus to Old Testament authors. These are called Messianic Prophecy (Messianic means about Jesus the Messiah and prophecy is a prediction). There are over 25 verses in the Old Testament that reference Jesus. Today, let's check out just a couple.

Read Micah 5:2.

This passage shows that Jesus has been since the beginning; He is eternal, or ancient. What city would this ancient ruler come from?

Week 1: The Word Became Flesh

Read Isaiah 7:14.

Who will give birth? (Remember this is a miracle in itself!)

What will He be called?

How should understanding that God knows the future affect how you live today?

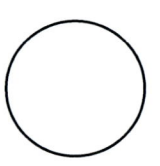

KIDS DAY 1

See this circle? Where does it begin? Where does it end? Just as a circle can go around and around forever without a beginning or end, God has always existed and will always exist, without a beginning or end. God has three parts: Father, Son, and Holy Spirit. The Son is Jesus. Did you know that Jesus existed even before He was born? He is just like this circle: He has always existed because He is God. In fact, the Bible tells us that through Jesus the whole world was made! Before Jesus came to earth as a baby, He was in Heaven with God the Father. The Bible calls Jesus the Word. When the Word became a person (Jesus), He came to earth to save us from our sins.

Memorize

"For God so loved the world that He gave His one and only son that whoever believes in Him shall not perish but have eternal life. For God did not send His son into the world to condemn the world but to save the world through Him." –John 3:16-17 NIV

For this and other long memory verses, feel free to focus on only part of the verse with young kids! You can always return to the study when they are older and learn more of the verse then.

Older Kids

Read John 1:1-18 in the NIrV.

Timeline

In the beginning, Jesus was the Word. Say "the Word" and hold your hands out in front of you, using your index fingers and thumbs to form a "W." Remember that Jesus is the Word who has always existed.

Pray

Try to pray with your kids at least once a day. It's great to have a balance of praying for them and praying with them as you guide them in how to pray. Need a model to use when praying with your kids? Try the one below. You say the start and have them fill in the blanks:

Thank you, God, for _____
Sorry for _____
Please help me _____
I pray for _____ (someone else)
In Jesus' name, amen.

Week 1: The Word Became Flesh

JUST FOR MOM

Read Luke 1:5-25.

What do we learn about John the Baptist? (Note: this is a different John than John the disciple.)

Read Luke 1:26-56.

What do we learn about Mary?

Look at verses 42-43. Elizabeth, a woman, is the first person to make a proclamation of faith that Jesus is LORD, and she does this before He is even born! What insight do verses 26-56 give you into God's view of women?

Mary was putting herself in a very dangerous position by saying yes to God. Having a baby out of wedlock could mean Joseph would divorce her, or worse, punishment by death. (Engagement in this time was much more serious than in our day... Even though they were only engaged, Joseph would have to divorce her if he did not follow through with their marriage.) Mary not only says "yes" to God, but she also responds with praise in verses 46-55.

What does today's reading teach me about how I should live?

KIDS DAY 2

Review the first step of our timeline, "the Word." Even before the creation of the world, God knew that Adam and Eve would sin and that one day Jesus, the Word, would become a human to save the world from sin. God knows the future and always has a plan. Sometimes, He tells people what will happen in advance. There are many places in the Old Testament of our Bibles, hundreds of years before the birth of Jesus, where God told human authors what to write about Jesus. This is called "prophecy." All the Old Testament prophecies about who would come to save people are fulfilled in Jesus... ALL OF THEM. Not one single prophecy was wrong! This should give us confidence that all of the Bible is true and that God is in control.

Timeline

Say "prophecy" and move your hand from your lips away from your mouth to represent speaking. God told the prophets what to say about Jesus, the Savior who would come to save His people.

**If you need assistance when reviewing our timeline, you can find the entire list in the Introduction.

Older Kids

Read Isaiah 53 in the NIrV to hear a prophecy about Jesus.

CHALLENGE FOR MOM

In the book of Matthew, the author focuses on how Jesus fulfilled Old Testament prophecy, proving to the Jews that He was the promised Messiah. Download a free audio Bible app and listen to the book of Matthew over the next two weeks.

Week 1: The Word Became Flesh

KIDS DAY 3

Review the timeline through "prophecy." What do you remember about the birth of Jesus? An angel appeared to a young woman named Mary and told her she would have a son. When the time came for Him to be born, Mary and Joseph were travelling to Bethlehem in obedience to a law that was issued by the ruler at that time. Remember how we talked last time about prophecy? In the Old Testament, there were prophecies that Jesus would be born in Bethlehem. Mary and Joseph didn't even live in Bethlehem! God moved them there by having the ruler decide to count all the people at just the right time, directing Joseph and his family to travel to Bethlehem for a census. Isn't that amazing how God was working out His plan?

Mary gave birth to Jesus and laid him in a manger, a feed trough for the animals. Meanwhile, angels appeared to shepherds nearby and told them about the birth of the Savior. The shepherds hurried to the manger to worship baby Jesus. After they saw Him, they went and shared the good news. God wants us to tell everyone about Jesus too! Who can you tell today that Jesus loves them and came to earth for them?

Timeline

Say "birth" and cradle your arms like you're holding a baby.

Older Kids

Read Luke 2:1-20 in the NIrV.

Week 2: Preparing for Ministry

Week 2: Preparing for Ministry

MOMS GROUP DISCUSSION

In preparing for ministry, Jesus learned and grew, studied Scripture, and was baptized. Finally, He was tempted in the wilderness before His public ministry began.

Read Matthew 4:1-11.

Jesus must have been very hungry and tired. He would have been weary and weak. What can we learn from Jesus' response to the first temptation?

What can we learn from Jesus' response to the second temptation?

What can we learn from Jesus' response to the third temptation?

What do Jesus' three responses to temptation all have in common? What does this teach us?

Since Jesus was tempted but never sinned, we can know that temptation is not a sin; it's only sin when we give in.

Read 1 Corinthians 10:13.

Often, we are ashamed of the things that tempt us, but this verse teaches that everything we're tempted with is common and that God will provide a way out. What is something that Satan has been using to tempt you? Where can you see a way out?

Read Hebrews 4:15-16.

What a comfort it is that Jesus, our High Priest, empathizes with our weakness! According to these verses, when we are tempted, or even if we fail, how should we respond? How will God respond?

KIDS DAY 1

Begin by reviewing the timeline through "birth." What do you think it was like for Jesus when He was your age? Can you believe He had to learn and do chores just like you? He gave up some of the rights of being God when He became a human and came to earth, so He needed to learn and study too. Jesus read God's Word and studied hard.

When Jesus was just a boy, He went to the temple and was asking the teachers such good questions that everyone was amazed by His understanding. Luke 2:52 says, "And Jesus grew in wisdom and stature, and in favor with God and man."

Jesus grew up, just like you're growing up. He grew wiser, taller, and impressed God and people because He did what was right. Let's pray now that you grow wiser, stronger, and more and more faithful to God!

Timeline

Say "growing" and take your hand from down low to way up high. Jesus had to learn and grow just like us!

Older Kids

Read Luke 2:41-52 in the NIrV.

JUST FOR MOM

Read Matthew 3:11-17.

Why do you think Jesus was baptized?

Week 2: Preparing for Ministry

Read Mark 1:4 and Acts 2:38.

Why should we be baptized?

Go to biblegateway.com. Search for "baptize." Read through all the times that "baptize" occurs in the book of Acts. Take notes on anything of interest here:

Now look at the final instance, Acts 22:16. Ask yourself this same question. If you have not been baptized as a result of faith in Christ, ask, "What am I waiting for?" Contact someone from your local church today to be baptized. If you have been baptized, who can you tell that story to?

KIDS DAY 2

Review the timeline through "growing." When Jesus had fully grown and was about 30 years old, God told Him it was time to start leading and teaching. Jesus' first step was an act of obedience: He needed to be baptized. Jesus went to the river where John was baptizing people and asked to be baptized as well. When Jesus had gone under the water and come back up, the Holy Spirit rested on His shoulder in the form of a dove, and a voice from Heaven (God the Father) said, "This is my son, whom I love. I'm very pleased with Him."

The Bible says we are to be baptized to express our faith in Jesus for the forgiveness of our sins and to receive the gift of the Holy Spirit. What happens when someone is baptized? Why should we get baptized? This is an important thing for you to pray about. When you feel God leading you to get baptized, we can talk to church leaders and take that step.

Timeline

Say "baptism," plug your nose, and lean backwards like you're being baptized.

Older Kids

Read Matthew 3:13-17 in the NIrV.

KIDS DAY 3

Review the timeline through "baptism." After Jesus was baptized, God directed Him to the desert to spend some time alone, praying and fasting (not eating) and getting ready to do ministry. After Jesus had been in the desert for 40 days, when He was very tired and hungry, Satan, the devil, came to Him and tried three times to tempt Him to sin.

Each time, Jesus used a Bible verse to combat Satan. That is why we memorize Bible verses, so we can use God's Word to help us do what's right. Psalm 119:11 says, "I have hidden your word in my heart that I might not sin against you." Jesus was tempted to sin, just like we are, but He never did. Jesus always did what was right.

Since Jesus was so hungry from not eating for 40 days, Satan tried to trick Him into turning some stones into bread. Jesus responds in Matthew 4:4, this week's memory verse.

Memorize

"Man shall not live on bread alone, but on every word that comes from the mouth of God." -Matthew 4:4

We will memorize this verse to help us remember that God's Word is EVEN MORE IMPORTANT for us than food! And just like we need to eat every day to grow our bodies strong, we need to read the Bible every day to grow strong in the Lord. Keep reading the Bible and practicing your memory verses so that you can use God's Word to help you stay away from sin and do what's right!

Timeline

Wiggle your arm like a snake slithering (since Satan appeared in Genesis as a snake) and say "temptation."

Older Kids

Read Matthew 4:1-11 in the NIrV.

Week 3: Miracles of Jesus

MOMS GROUP DISCUSSION

Jesus did many miracles in His time on earth. We will focus on just a few over the next two weeks.

Read Mark 5:22-34.

What was Jesus' mission? (What had Jairus asked him to do?)

What "distraction" came during His mission?

How did Jesus respond?

Jesus took time for this woman. Often we see distractions and interruptions as unpleasant and unwanted, perhaps missing a wonderful opportunity God has placed before us.

Tell about a distraction or interruption that came this week. How did you respond? What was the result?

Jesus took time for this woman to show her she was valued and loved. How can you remind yourself to take time away from your "plan" to show your kids and your spouse they're valued and loved?

How can you welcome God's interruptions into your day so that you can be His instrument of blessing for others?

Week 3: Miracles of Jesus

KIDS DAY 1

Review the timeline through "temptation." After Jesus' temptation in the desert, He began His ministry of teaching and healing. He called 12 men to be His disciples and closest friends, walking alongside Him and learning from Him. The word "disciple" means student. These 12 disciples followed Jesus almost everywhere He went to learn from Him. They saw Him perform miracles and heard Him teach.

Do you know what a miracle is? It's a surprising event that can't be explained by science. It's something good that couldn't just happen on its own. Jesus did many miracles in His time on earth.

Timeline

Say "miracles" and open your arms big and wide. We're going to learn 5 of Jesus' many miracles in our timeline.

Option: Grab a blanket or sheet (blue if possible), a toy boat or a light object like a tissue box to represent the boat, a portable fan, and a spray bottle of water. Place the blanket on the floor with the "boat" in the middle. Have one child spray water when you mention rain in the story below, and another child make waves by lifting and shaking the blanket like a parachute when we say "waves." You could even add a fan on "high" for wind!

Since Jesus was fully God and fully human, He had the power to control even the wind and the waves. Imagine the most wind you've ever felt. If you had said, "Stop wind," what would happen? Nothing, right? The wind won't listen to us, but it does listen to Jesus.

One day, Jesus and His 12 disciples were on a boat in the middle of a lake. A storm came up that was so strong, the disciples thought they were going to drown. The wind blew (cue fan), the rain poured down (squirt the spray bottle), and the waves crashed over the boat (bring on the waves)! The disciples thought for sure they would drown. But where was Jesus? He was asleep! "Wake up teacher!" they yelled at Him. "Don't you care if we drown?" Jesus got up and said to them, "You have such little faith." Then, He said to the wind and waves, "Quiet, be still," and all was calm. His disciples were surprised and said, "Who is this? Even the wind and the waves obey Him!" *(You can have your kids take turns creating the wind, waves, and rain and calming them by saying "Be still.")*

Timeline

Say "storm" and spread your arms out like Jesus reaching out to calm the wind and the waves. Jesus calmed the storm and can control the weather and the sea! Thank God that He is powerful and can control all of nature.

Jesus was sad that His disciples were so scared. They didn't have faith to trust Him to care for them. Will you trust God the next time you're afraid? This week's memory verse will help us remember to trust God.

Memorize

John 14:1, "Don't let your hearts be troubled. Trust in God, and trust also in me."

Older Kids

Read Mark 4:35-41 in the NIrV.

JUST FOR MOM

There are four books of the Bible that tell about the life of Jesus. These are called the Gospels, and they include the books of Matthew, Mark, Luke, and John. Many of the same stories are found throughout the Gospels, but different authors chose to emphasize different things. Mark put a heavy emphasis on Jesus' miracles.

The Gospel of Mark was written by John Mark. Though he was not one of the 12 disciples, this was probably the first Gospel to be written. The three other Gospels quote all but 31 verses of Mark. Throughout this week and next, your challenge is to listen to all of Mark. (You can search your app store for "free audio Bible" for options.) Listen while you drive, cook, and clean. Meditate on God's Word throughout your day. As you listen, ask yourself the three W's: What does it say? What does it teach me about God? What does it teach me about how I should live? If possible, keep notes in a journal, or use the space at the end of this chapter.

Week 3: Miracles of Jesus

KIDS DAY 2

Practice the timeline up through "storm." One day, a religious leader came to Jesus because his daughter was sick. He asked Jesus to make her well. Jesus agreed to go with him but got stopped by a woman who needed help. As Jesus was talking to her, the leader's servants came to tell him his daughter had died. When Jesus heard this, He told the father not to fear, but to have faith. Jesus went with him and told the dead girl to get up. Immediately, she got up and was well again! It's important for us to have faith like the religious leader, to ask God for help, and to keep believing!

Timeline

Say "child" and take your arm from horizontal (representing that she was laying down, dead) and raise it up to vertical (to represent her getting up and being well).

Older Kids

Read Mark 5:21-43 in the NIrV.

Week 4: Miracles Part 2

Week 4: Miravles Part 2

MOMS GROUP DISCUSSION

Read Luke 5:18-26.

In verse 20, what did Jesus see?

What did He do as a result?

Let's not miss this! The faith of this man's friends brought him forgiveness of sins, and in result, right-standing with God. We don't know if this paralytic had faith of his own or not, but his friends had enough faith for him!

Share about a time when someone else's faith strengthened your faith in Christ.

This right here is the importance of group discussion and learning in community. We are here for one another, to be strong when someone else is weak, to strengthen each other and pull one another along. Silent reflection: Who from this group can you reach out to this week to encourage? How will you do it?

Read James 5:16-20.

How will we carry one another's burdens as a group?

How will we respond when someone confronts us in love?

KIDS DAY 1

Review the timeline up through "child." One day, as Jesus was teaching, some men brought their friend who couldn't walk to be healed by Jesus. But the crowds were so big they could not get their friend to Jesus. Back in this time, homes were built with stairs up onto the roof, which was kind of like a deck on a house today. These friends carried the paralyzed man up onto the roof and started pulling the roof apart! They made a hole and lowered their friend down through the roof to Jesus. When Jesus saw their faith, He said to the paralytic, "Your sins are forgiven." Then, so that everyone knew Jesus truly had the power to forgive sins, He also said, "Get up and walk."

Immediately, the man got up and walked! Jesus can heal us physically (our bodies) AND spiritually (from our sins). This man was forgiven of his sins because of the faith of his friends. What friends could you help bring to Jesus? What are some steps you can take this week to do that? (Ideas: invite them to church, ask them if they believe in God, or pray for them.) Jesus wants us to have big faith like these friends!

Memorize

Matthew 21:21 "...You must have faith and not doubt..."

Timeline

Pretend that you're pulling a roof apart like the friends did and say "roof."

Older Kids

Read Luke 5:12-26 in the NIrV.

JUST FOR MOM

Continue last week's assignment to listen to all of Mark. Listen while you drive, cook, and clean. Meditate on God's Word throughout your day. When you've finished, sit down and journal about the book as a whole, considering the big picture.

Week 4: Miracles Part 2

Answer the 3 W's about the overall story of Mark:
What does it say?

What does it teach me about God?

What does it teach me about how to live?

KIDS DAY 2

Review the timeline up through "roof." Just like there was a huge crowd surrounding Jesus when these men brought their paralyzed friend and lowered him through the roof, there were often large crowds following Jesus. One day, as He and His disciples were getting out of a boat, they saw a huge crowd had gathered to hear Him teach. As it grew later in the day, Jesus' disciples came to Him and said, "Let's send these people away so they can get food." Jesus responded, "You feed them." The disciples couldn't believe it! This would cost too much money and they wouldn't know where to get enough food for such a large crowd: there were 5000 men there, and that doesn't even count women and children! That's a lot of people to feed!

Jesus asked, "What food do you have?" The disciples found 5 loaves of bread and 2 fish that one boy had packed. Jesus took that little amount of food, looked to Heaven and thanked His Father, then broke the bread. He had the disciples pass it out, and amazingly there was enough to feed everyone and 12 baskets leftover!

Timeline

Jesus fed many more than 5000 people, because it was 5000 men and their families, but this miracle is commonly known as the feeding of 5000. Say "5000 fed" and with each syllable, use your hand to show five fingers, zero, zero, zero. Remember that this many men and their families were fed with just 5 little loaves of bread and 2 small fish. What a miracle!

Older Kids

Read Mark 6:30-44 in the NIrV.

KIDS DAY 3

Review the timeline up through "5000 fed." Right after Jesus fed over 5000 families, He told His disciples to get in a boat and go across the lake so He could have some alone time to pray. It is SO IMPORTANT to spend time alone with God praying! When do you pray? If Jesus needed to pray, so do we!

In the middle of the night, the disciples were still in the boat out on the lake when they were caught in a strong wind and couldn't get to shore. Jesus knew they were in trouble (He knows everything!), so He came to them walking on the water across the lake. They were terrified (I would be too if I saw someone walking on the water AND it was dark and stormy!), but Jesus said, "Be brave! It's me!" Peter responded, "Lord, if it's really you, tell me to walk on the water to you." Brave Peter. Would you be brave enough to get out of the boat and walk to Jesus?

Jesus said, "Come." Peter stepped out of the boat and began to walk on the water, but he stopped focusing on Jesus, became afraid, and began to sink. He cried out for help. Jesus grabbed him and helped him into the boat. He said to Peter, "Your faith is so small." Peter had more faith than the other 11 disciples because he DID get out of the boat, but his faith was so little that he began to doubt and sink. When is your faith in Jesus big and strong? Are there areas where you feel like your faith is too small, like Peter's?

Timeline

Say "walks on water" and move two fingers like they are legs walking.

Older Kids

Read Matthew 14:22-36 in the NIrV.

29

Week 5: Parables of Jesus

MOMS GROUP DISCUSSION

Jesus often taught in parables, stories that are used to illustrate a point. Over the next two weeks, we will dive into a handful of the many parables He used. This week, we are focusing on the parables of the lost.

Read Luke 15:1-7.

Look at verses 1-2. What are the Pharisees upset about?

Do you ever find yourself in this mode of thinking, either judging who others hang out with or determining someone is "too sinful" for you to spend time with?

Jesus tells the parable of the lost sheep (verses 3-7) in response to the hearts of the Pharisees. How is the church (not necessarily your church, but the worldwide Church or Christians in general) sometimes like the Pharisees?

What do you think Jesus wants Christians and His Church to learn from the parable in verses 3-7?

How do you need to live differently because of this parable?

Week 5: Parables of Jesus

KIDS DAY 1

Review the timeline up through "walks on water."

Timeline

When Jesus taught the people, He often used stories to illustrate His point and teach a lesson. These stories are called "parables." Put your hands together, palms up like a book, since these are stories (even though He told them out loud), and say "parables."

Jesus taught several parables about the lost. We're going to look at a few of them this week. When Jesus was surrounded by sinners, the religious leaders, called Pharisees, criticized Him. They thought that truly religious people shouldn't be with those who don't live "good" lives. In response, Jesus told this parable about sheep and a shepherd:

If a shepherd has 100 sheep and he loses one, he will leave the 99 to go look for that one lost sheep. And when he finds it, he will throw a party because his sheep was lost and is now found. Then Jesus explained that in the same way, when someone who doesn't yet believe in God believes and is sorry for their sin, there is happiness and celebration in Heaven! God is even more excited about lost people getting saved than "good" people making sure to do everything right.

Jesus cares this much about making sure you follow Him as well. He wants you to believe in Him, turn from your sins (stop choosing your own way rather than obeying God) and follow Him. He will keep coming after you like the shepherd searched for that lost sheep because He loves you so much!

Memorize

Luke 19:10, "For the Son of Man came to seek and to save the lost."

Jesus sometimes referred to Himself as the "Son of Man" to show His humanity. Even though Jesus is fully God, He became fully human to live on earth like us. Jesus came to earth because He cares about you and me. He came so He could find you and be your friend!

Older Kids

Read Luke 15:1-10 the NIrV.

JUST FOR MOM

Read Luke 15:11-32.

In what ways are you like the young man who squanders his wealth?

In what ways are you like the angry brother, upset at his father's forgiveness? How has God acted like this father to you in your life?

How will you live differently because of this parable?

CHALLENGE FOR MOM

The Gospel of Luke is the only Gospel written by a Gentile (a non-Jew). Luke was a physician. In addition to writing Luke, he wrote the book of Acts about the early church. Luke focuses on Jesus' perfect humanity. He was fully God and fully man. Luke emphasises how Jesus was a man who never sinned and how He taught the people powerfully. Pull out your audio Bible app and listen to the book of Luke over the next two weeks.

Week 5: Parables of Jesus

KIDS DAY 2

Review the timeline up through "parables." Jesus told another parable to tell how important it is to bring lost people (those who don't know Jesus) to believe in Him. This is the parable of the prodigal, or wandering, son:

One day, a son came to his father and said, "Give me the money that I would get if you died; I want it now." This made the father sad, but he gave his son the money. The son went away and spent all his money on silly things: parties, food, and wild living. When his money ran out, he didn't even have anything to eat or any place to sleep. He decided to go work as a helper on a farm, caring for pigs. He got so hungry, he even ate the pig food! Finally, he realized that even his father's servants eat better than this. So he went home, planning to tell his dad he was sorry for his bad choices and to beg his forgiveness. But his father saw him coming and ran to him. He hugged him, welcomed him, and threw a huge party because he was so happy to have his son back.

If you ever mess up, God will be waiting for you to come back to Him, ready to forgive you and throw a party because He loves you! He also wants everyone else to come back to Him too! How can you lead others who are not following God to come back to Him?

Timeline

Hold your hand above your eyes and look around you, like you're the father scanning around for the return of his lost son or the shepherd looking for the lost sheep and say, "lost."

Older Kids

Read Luke 15:11-32 in the NIrV.

Week 6: Parables Part 2

Week 6: Parables Part 2

MOMS GROUP DISCUSSION

Read Matthew 13:24-30.

What do you learn from this parable of the weeds?

Read Matthew 13:34-43.

What insight does this give you to the "here and now" life on this earth?

What insight does this parable give us to the future, the end of earth, and eternity in Heaven or Hell?

How should we live differently because of this teaching?

KIDS DAY 1

Review the timeline up through "lost." One day, Jesus told a parable about 4 different types of soil for planting seeds:

A farmer went out and scattered seeds. Some seed fell on the path, and birds came and ate it up. That represents those who hear about God and don't understand. Satan comes and snatches the truth away. Some seed fell on rocky ground. It sprang up quickly because the soil was shallow, but then when the sun came, the plants withered because their roots weren't deep. This illustrates someone who receives God's Word with joy, but when trouble comes, he falls away because he is not rooted deeply. Other seed fell among thorns, which grew up and choked the plants. This symbolizes the one who hears the word, but the worries of this life and the desire for money and "stuff" choke it out. Other seed fell on good soil and produced a great crop. This represents those who hear God's Word and understand it. When we read the Bible and go to church, we can pray that God's Holy Spirit will help us to understand God's Word and live it out so that we can be this good soil, producing great "crops" for God!

Timeline

Pretend to scatter seed on the ground and say, "4 soils." Let's remember to be the good soil to hear God's Word and obey it!

Memorize

"I am the vine. You are the branches. If you remain joined to me, and I to you, you will bear a lot of fruit. You can't do anything without me." -John 15:5

How can you remain joined to Jesus? We want to be the good soil or the branch that produces a lot of fruit, but we can't do that alone. We need to daily ask Jesus for help. Let's stay connected to Him, talking to Him throughout the day.

Pray

Every time you're about to read the Bible, begin the habit of praying FIRST that God would give you understanding for what you read to help you be the good soil from this parable.

Older Kids

Read Matthew 13:1-23 in the NIrV.

JUST FOR MOM

Begin by praying that the Holy Spirit would help you to understand God's Word and apply it in your life.

Read Matthew 13:44-46.

How does your desire for Jesus compare to the value you place on the things of this world?

Week 6: Parables Part 2

📖 Read Matthew 13:47-50.

Does your life reflect that you believe there will come a time where Jesus separates those who follow Him from those who don't?

Jesus talks about separating the wicked from the righteous. But we know that there is no one who is righteous on their own. Let's check out Jesus' discussion with a rich man who did his best to be "good" and keep all the commandments.

📖 Read Matthew 19:16-30.

Why wasn't keeping the commands enough for this man?

What do you hold so dearly that it's keeping you from Jesus?

Spend some time in prayer, surrendering everything to God and declaring He is number one in your life.

KIDS DAY 2

Review the timeline up through "4 soils." One day, an expert in the law questioned Jesus on what it takes to receive eternal life. Jesus asked, "What is written in the law?" The man responded, "Love the Lord your God with all your heart and love your neighbor as yourself." Jesus replied, "You have answered correctly. Do this and you will live." But the man continued, "Who is my neighbor?" In response, Jesus told him this parable:

A man was walking down the road when some robbers attacked him. They beat him and left him on the side of the road badly injured. A priest (or pastor) came by a little later, but he avoided the injured man and continued along on the other side of the road. Next, an expert of the law came and also passed by. But a Samaritan (a person who would have been treated poorly in this time and wasn't thought of very highly), stopped, helped the man, and took him to an inn where he could be safe and heal.

Jesus pointed out that it was this Samaritan, not the really "religious" people, who acted like a neighbor. Jesus told this story to show us that everyone is our neighbor. We are to treat every person, whether poor or rich, kind or mean, good or evil, with the same kind of love and respect that we would want given to us.

Timeline

Pretend you're wrapping a big bandage around your arm and say "Good Samaritan" to represent how the Good Samaritan showed love and kindness by helping the hurt man.

Memorize

"You must love the Lord your God with all your heart, all your soul, and all your mind. This is the first and greatest commandment. A second is equally important: Love your neighbor as yourself."
-Matthew 22: 37-39 NLT

Jesus said all the commands can be summed up into two. The parable of the Good Samaritan teaches us how to keep the second command of loving our neighbor.

Older Kids

Read Luke 10:25-37 in the NIrV.

39

Week 7: Teachings of Jesus

MOMS GROUP DISCUSSION

Matthew chapters 5-7 contain some powerful, perspective-shifting teaching from Jesus. This portion of Scripture is known as the Sermon on the Mount. We will be spending a lot of time here this week. The end of chapter 4 sets the stage and provides the context for this sermon, which was more likely the compilation of Jesus' teaching over several days, rather than a 40-minute sermon like we hear at church.

Read Matthew 4:23-5:2 and Matthew 6:19-24.

How are you tempted to store up treasure on earth?

Do you ever feel your heart is divided between God and money? How so?

What can we do to be sure we're serving God rather than money or earthly treasure?

Read Matthew 6:25-34.

Why shouldn't we worry? (Hint: see verses 27 and 33.)

How can we actively stop worrying?

Memory for Mom

Matthew 6:21, 24b, 27, and 33-34 are great memory verses for mom! Post them on your mirror or in your car where you can see and meditate on them this week.

Week 7: Teachings of Jesus

KIDS DAY 1

Review the timeline through "Good Samaritan." Jesus taught a lot through parables, but He also had many other teachings as well, which we'll learn about this week.

Timeline

Say "teachings" and pretend to write on a dry erase board like a teacher teaching at the front of the classroom.

One time, Jesus taught many things to a crowd on the side of a mountain. This is called the Sermon on the Mount, and it is a great summary of the life Jesus wants us to live.

Timeline

Put your hands together on top of your head forming a mountain peak and say "Sermon on the Mount."

In the Sermon on the Mount, Jesus starts with many sayings about who will be blessed. Jesus tells us in Matthew 5:9 that we'll be blessed and happy if we are a peacemaker. What do you think it means to be a peacemaker? How can you be a peacemaker in your house? This is our memory verse for the week, and we're going to work really hard on doing all we can to bring peace and settle conflict, not create or aggravate it!

Memorize

"Blessed are the peacemakers, for they will be called children of God."
-Matthew 5:9 NIV

Older Kids

Read Matthew 5:1-12 in the NIrV.

JUST FOR MOM

Take some time to read through the Sermon on the Mount. Ask the Holy Spirit to teach you as you read. Take notes or highlight in your Bible any teachings that stand out to you.

Read Matthew chapters 5-7.

What does Jesus say about:

ANGER

LUST/DIVORCE

VOWS

RETALIATION/ENEMIES

GIVING

Week 7: Teachings of Jesus

PRAYER

FASTING

MONEY

WORRY

CRITICIZING

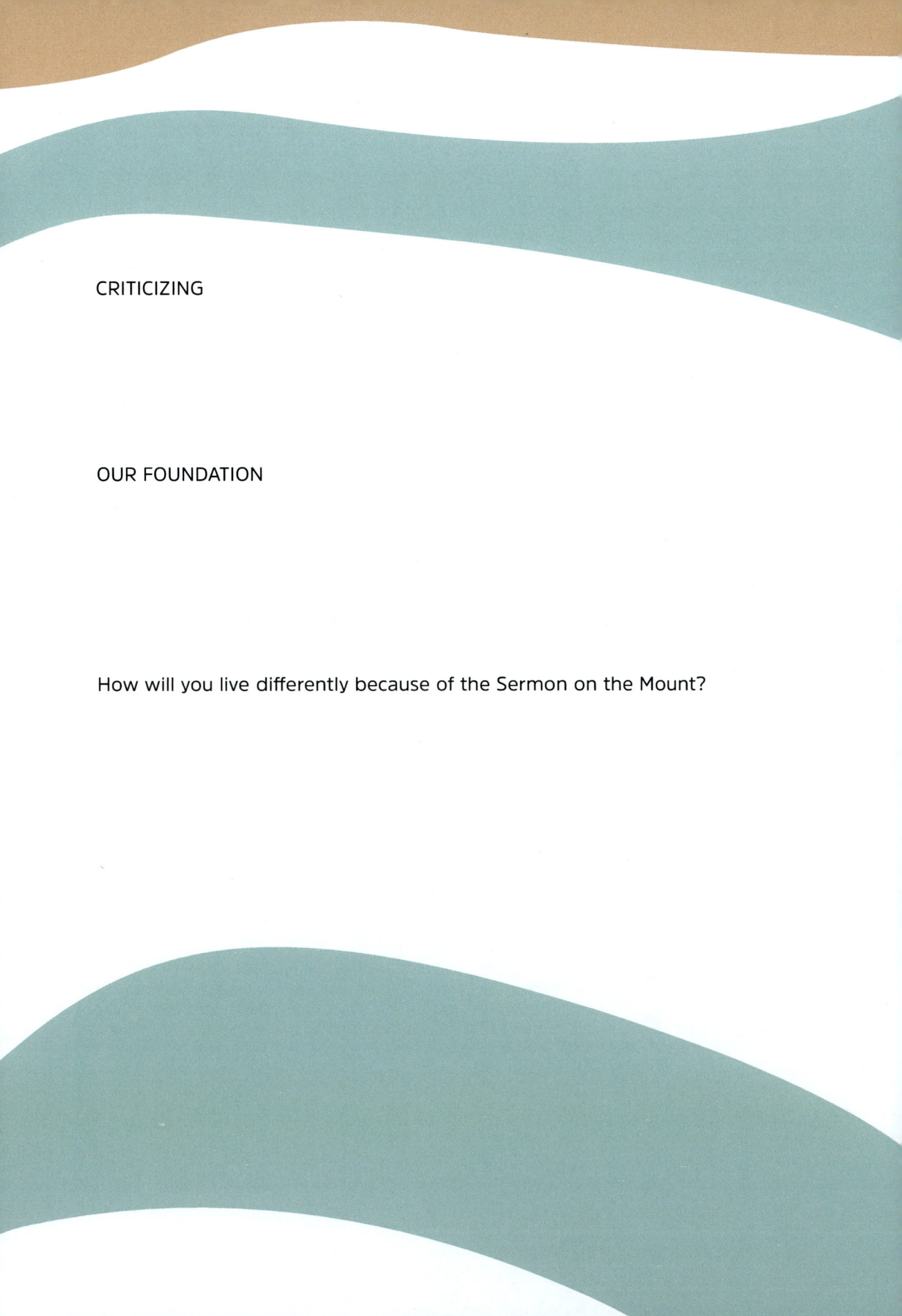

OUR FOUNDATION

How will you live differently because of the Sermon on the Mount?

Week 7: Teachings of Jesus

KIDS DAY 2

Review the timeline up through "Sermon on the Mount." Today we're going to learn more of what Jesus taught in the Sermon on the Mount. Jesus says that we are the light of the world, and in Matthew 5:16 He continues, "Let your light shine before others, that they may see your good deeds and praise your Father in Heaven." What does it mean to let your light shine? Hint: your light is your love for Jesus.

In John 8:12, Jesus says, "I am the light of the world." We are also the light when we have Jesus inside of us and we reflect His light to the world. Why do we want to shine His goodness and love? Because others will see it and glorify God. We are here on earth to know God and make Him known to others. We must not be afraid to be different or to be the only ones following God, because that's how we lead others to Him!

Jesus also talks in the Sermon on the Mount about how we are to get along with others. He teaches that if someone hurts us, we are not to hurt them back. If someone takes something that belongs to us, we don't take something of theirs or try to get even. Instead, we still show them love and kindness. We forgive and we pray for others even when they're mean to us!

Older Kids

Read Matthew 5:38-48 and 6:14-15 in the NIrV.

KIDS DAY 3

Review the timeline through "Sermon on the Mount." Near the end of the Sermon on the Mount, Jesus tells the people how important it is to build your life on Jesus and nothing else. We might think that money, or having lots of friends, or being really smart are what matter, but in the end, all of those things don't really matter at all. What matters more than anything in this whole world is believing in Jesus and following Him. Are you committed to follow Jesus no matter what? I am!

Older Kids

Read Matthew 7:21-29 in the NIrV.

Week 8: Teachings Part 2

Week 8: Teachings Part 2

MOMS GROUP DISCUSSION

This week we are continuing in the teachings of Jesus, and today we will focus on prayer in Luke 11.

Read Luke 11:1.

What do you notice about Jesus?

Jesus was modelling the necessity of prayer for His disciples through His lifestyle! Do you model the necessity of prayer for your kids? If so, how?

It also seemed Jesus had a specific place (or maybe more than one) that He liked to go pray. Do you have a special prayer place?

What do you notice about the disciples?

Note that the disciples say, "Teach us to pray," not "Teach us how to pray." They want the kind of prayer life Jesus has! And they know that it's the act of praying that is most important, not how you pray. Do you ever get hung up on how to pray, so much so that it hinders you from even beginning?

Read Luke 11:2-4.

Does this sound familiar to you? This passage is often referred to as The Lord's Prayer. It is a model for prayer that Jesus gave us. Jesus demonstrates praising God, asking for our needs, asking for forgiveness, forgiving others, and staying away from sin. In keeping with this example, many people use the ACTS model to guide their prayers. I've simplified this for use with kids to the model provided in Week 1, which we will revisit in the Kids' portion this week.

**ADORATION
CONFESSION
THANKSGIVING
SUPPLICATION (ASKING)**

Notice Jesus spends just 3 verses teaching His disciples how to pray. Now, He spends the next 9 verses teaching them *to* pray, reinforcing that *how* is not the important part, actually praying is!

Read Luke 11:5-13.

In verse 8, why does the friend finally answer?

What is Jesus' message in verse 10?

What can verses 11-13 teach us about how God answers our prayers?

God is a good and loving Father. He wants us to come to Him over and over again... He won't get sick of it! The Greek in verse 9 literally means "ask and keep asking." Come to Him. Constantly. Lay your worries and burdens before Him. And here's the amazing part: God will lovingly give you what is best! He may answer differently than how we want or expect because He knows what is better. He also promises to give His Holy Spirit for wisdom and comfort.

Jesus wants us to see God as our loving Father who desires a relationship with us. He shows us that it is most important simply to talk to Him and that we shouldn't worry about saying the exact right thing in the exact right way. What will you change about your prayer life as a result of today's study?

Week 8: Teachings Part 2

KIDS DAY 1

Review the timeline through "Sermon on the Mount." Jesus taught us many things. One thing He taught about was prayer. He taught His disciples that God is their loving Father who wants to spend time with them. God wants us to talk to Him about anything, anytime, and in any way. There is no right or wrong way to pray. Do you feel comfortable praying and talking to God? Why or why not? What can our family do to make you more comfortable?

Here's a model that we can use to guide our prayers because it reminds us of some of the things that are important to pray about. But we don't always have to follow this model. We can talk to God from our heart, just like we talk to a friend. Let's try the model prayer, and then let's just talk to God afterwards about anything you want. Ready?

Thank You, God, for _____
Sorry for _____
Please help me _____
I pray for _____
I just want to talk to you about _____

Timeline

Say "pray" and put your hands together in front of your chest like some people do to pray. Since we can pray anytime and any way, we don't have to fold our hands or close our eyes, but that often helps take away distractions and keeps us focused on God.

Older Kids

Read Luke 11:1-13 in the NIrV.

JUST FOR MOM

The Gospel of John is perhaps the most personal of all four Gospels. It was written by the disciple John, who was arguably Jesus' closest friend. John refers to himself in his Gospel as "the disciple Jesus loved." That's all the identity he needed: to be loved by Jesus! Because of John's closeness to Jesus, this Gospel is intensely personal.

It is only fitting that we go here as we begin to bring our study to a close, examining Jesus' relationships with people and the events of Holy Week (the week of Jesus' crucifixion and resurrection).

For the other Gospels, I suggested you listen to an audio version. For this one, I ask that you sit and be with the text. Experience it. Read about Jesus as if you were reading an account of a new best friend. We will take 4 weeks to go through John, which works out to less than a chapter a day, but go at whatever pace you need.

Read John 1.

What do you learn about Jesus' relationship with:
God the Father:

The disciples:

Read John 2.

What do you learn about Jesus' relationship with:
His mother:

His Heavenly Father:

Read John 3.

What does this story teach you about Nicodemus?

What does it teach you about how you should live?

Week 8: Teachings Part 2

📖 *Read John 4.*

What do you learn about Jesus from His interactions with this woman at the well?

What does this teach you about how you should live?

What do you learn from the story of the Roman official?

KIDS DAY 2

Review the timeline up through "pray." Jesus went all around teaching and healing. Crowds often followed Him. Matthew 9:36-38 says, "When he saw the crowds, he felt deep concern for them. They were treated badly and were helpless, like sheep without a shepherd. Then Jesus said to his disciples, 'The harvest is huge. But there are only a few workers. So ask the Lord of the harvest to send workers out into his harvest field.'" Jesus was sad because the people were lost and in desperate need of Him. He felt the weight of the responsibility of telling everyone that He was the way to God, and He knew He couldn't do it alone. That's why Jesus tells the disciples to ask God to send more workers.

In farming, if a harvest is ripe it means the food is ready. Pumpkins, apples, berries, and corn all are ripe and ready to be picked. Have you ever picked fruits or vegetables? How do you know something is ripe? Jesus says that the harvest for people is ripe. It is God's Holy Spirit Who works on the hearts of lost people to draw them to Him. Since Jesus says the harvest is ripe, God is actively working on the hearts of the lost. Now He wants willing workers to go gather the harvest. That means people like us who know that Jesus is the way to God need to go tell others about Him. Do you ever talk to people about

God? Why or why not? Why do you think Jesus wants us to talk to others about Him?

Here are some ideas of how you can be one of these workers that Jesus asked to help with the harvest:

-Invite others to church.
-Ask your friends if they believe in Jesus or in Heaven.
-Talk about Jesus every day. For instance, saying, "I'm so thankful Jesus gave me you as a friend."
-Talk with your friends about what you learn at church or when you read the Bible.
-Tell others (friends, relatives, etc.) that Jesus loves them and wants to be their friend.
-Pray for people you know who don't believe in Jesus to know Him and to be "ripe" for the harvest!
-Living a life that pleases Jesus by doing what is right and good and kind helps lead others to Him. This is a way we can shine our light, like we learn about in this week's memory verse.

Memorize

"In the same way, let your light shine before others, that they may see your good deeds and glorify your Father in heaven." -Matthew 5:16

Timeline

Act like you're picking fruits or vegetables and say "harvest."

Older Kids

Make a list of people you know that you're not sure believe in Jesus. Start praying over this list every day and try to talk about Jesus when you're around these people. Take some time to pray over that list right now.

Week 9:
Jesus and People

MOMS GROUP DISCUSSION

Turn to John 4. Here we have one of my favorite encounters Jesus has with a woman.

Read John 4:1-6.

Jesus didn't "have to" go through Samaria because it was the only way to get where He was going. In fact, because Jews despised Samaritans, it was much more common for them to take a different route. Jesus "had to" go to Samaria because He had a divine appointment with this woman. Jesus was willing to alter His travel plans for this one woman He needed to meet.

Are you flexible and open to the changes Jesus brings to your plans? Have you noticed a "divine interruption" in your life before? (This is a time that God intervened and changed your plans because He had something else intended for you.)

The Gospel of John shows a marvelous picture of how fully God and how fully human Jesus is. Look back at verse 6. Even Jesus got tired and weary; even He would want a break on that 10-hour family road trip! Whatever we go through, Jesus gets it, because He has experienced it. Don't miss this or pass the chance to be in awe of our Creator: fully God and fully human.

Why do you think it's important that Jesus subjected Himself to human suffering, shame, sadness, fatigue, and hunger?

How does this make Christ more personal to you?

Read John 4:7-15.

This woman was at the well at noon, the 6th hour, the hottest part of the day. Most women went to draw water in the early morning, but her questionable lifestyle left her coming at the time where she was least likely to encounter anyone else. Of course she longed for Jesus to fulfil her immediate earthly desire to have endless water so she wouldn't have to keep coming to the well in fatigue and fear!

Week 9: Jesus and People

Read John 4:16-19 and 25-30.

Jesus shows He knows her deepest, darkest secrets, and then proclaims He is the Messiah. Immediately she leaves her water jars (forget about that physical need for water that troubled her earlier!) and she goes to tell others about Jesus. One of the greatest sinners has become one of the first female evangelists!

What are you holding onto that sometimes keeps you from sharing Jesus with others?

Notice the disciples are surprised to find Jesus talking to a woman. The Greek word used here means not only to be surprised, but to have awe or admiration. In the culture Christ was born into, men did not talk to women in public. Jesus not only breaks this social norm to show this sinner her worth, but He places Himself in need of her help. Jesus sat on the well with no bucket with which to draw water. *He* needed *her* before He points out *her* need for *Him*. Jesus came as a humble servant, and throughout His life He continually lifted women up. In a society that said women were full of shame and had very little worth, Jesus constantly lifted women up and restored the value He intended at creation, and the disciples were in awe of this.

Read John 4:39-42.

What a perfect picture of evangelism! We are to tell others about Jesus so they can meet Him for themselves and discover who He truly is. What touches you about this story?

What challenges you about this story?

KIDS DAY 1

Review the timeline through "harvest." One of the disciples Jesus called to follow Him was Matthew, the tax collector. The Jews hated tax collectors because they had to pay so much money in taxes to Rome, and the tax collectors were often dishonest, making people pay even more than what they owed.

One day, Matthew hosted a dinner. Jesus was there, and so were other tax collectors and people who were known to lead sinful lives. The religious teachers of this time (Pharisees) saw Jesus and criticized Him for eating with sinners. The Pharisees wouldn't spend time with these people because they thought they were too good for them. But Jesus responded, "It is not the healthy who need a doctor, but the sick." He was trying to teach them that those who are "sick" with sin are those who need God's help the most. We need to remember that Jesus loves everyone, and all people deserve to hear about His love.

Timeline

Say "eats with sinners" and pretend to spoon food into your mouth. This is a reminder that we should be kind to everyone and that even people who are not like us or who make bad choices need to hear about Jesus. We need to show God's love and kindness to everyone.

Memorize

"By this everyone will know that you are my disciples, if you love one another." -John 13:35

Older Kids

Read Matthew 9:10-13 in the NIrV

JUST FOR MOM

We're going to continue reading in John, experiencing Jesus afresh and anew. As you read, keep your focus on His relationships with people.

Read John 5.

What do you learn about Jesus' relationship with His Father?

Read John 6.

What do you learn about who Jesus is?

Week 9: Jesus and People

What do you learn about how Jesus cares for His people?

What is your daily bread? How will you get it?

Read John 7.

What do you learn about Jesus' relationship with the religious leaders?

How does His teaching for them apply to you also?

Read John 8.

What do you learn about Jesus from His interactions with the adulterous woman?

What do you learn about judging?

What evidence do you find in the text that Jesus is God and that He has always existed?

Read John 9.

What do you learn about Jesus from His interaction with the blind man?

Where are you spiritually blind?

Read John 10.

What do you learn about your Good Shepherd and His relationship with all believers, His sheep?

KIDS DAY 2

Review the timeline up through "eats with sinners." Jesus had some friends named Mary, Martha, and their brother Lazarus. Jesus came to their home one day, and Mary sat at Jesus' feet and listened while Martha was busy cleaning and preparing food. Martha got frustrated and said to Jesus, "Make Mary help me! There's so much work to do!" But Jesus responded gently, "Martha, you're worried about many things, but Mary has chosen what is greater."

Often we get caught up in the things we do: who's the best at something, what we can accomplish, or even just staying busy and having fun. But Jesus taught the importance of being still and spending time with Him. To sit and listen to Jesus is one of the best things we can do. How can you be still and learn from Jesus?

When we do this study together, reading, learning Bible verses, and doing our timeline, we are taking time to sit and learn from Jesus. It's so important, and I'm glad we can do this together!

Timeline

Say "Mary and Martha" and hold one hand palm up to one side, then the other hand palm up to the other side, like you're comparing these women's actions. Martha was doing a good thing, but the best choice we can make is to be a disciple of Jesus, taking time to learn from Him.

Older Kids

Read Luke 10:38-42 in the NIrV.

Week 10: Holy Week

MOMS GROUP DISCUSSION

Hopefully you've been working through the Gospel of John in the "Just for Mom" portion of this study. We're about halfway through, and there begins to be a shift in the book. John 11 foreshadows Jesus' death and introduces the plot to have Him killed. John 12-20 recounts the events of just one week, often referred to as "Holy Week." John 13-17 takes place on the night of what many call "The Last Supper." The time was near for the Passover feast, a celebration of when God delivered His people from slavery in Egypt and they were saved by the blood of a pure, spotless lamb. (For background on the Passover, see Exodus 12.) Little did the disciples know, as they approached the Passover this year, Jesus, the pure spotless lamb in human form, was about to deliver them and all mankind from slavery to sin and death!

At the Last Supper, Jesus washes His disciples' feet, the ultimate sign of servitude. Then, He speaks to them with important instructions, His final words of His ministry on earth. Let's listen in.

Read John 14:1-6.

Why shouldn't they worry or fear?

What is Jesus doing for them (and us) now?

How do we get to Heaven to be with Him?

Read John 15:1-5.

How can you remain, or abide, in Christ?

Why is it important that we abide in Him?

Week 10: Holy Week

This week's "JUST FOR MOM" section has you reading through the first part of Holy Week in John 13-17. Even if you do no other homework for the rest of this study, do this week's "JUST FOR MOM." These are Jesus' words in His final hours. If you knew you had only a few hours left to live, you'd make sure to convey whatever was most important to you, right? There is so much wealth in John 13-17 that we could spend a whole session here. Take some time. Dig in. Allow God to speak to you through the Holy Spirit, Who is in you, as you study this week.

KIDS DAY 1

Review the timeline through "Mary and Martha." When Jesus knew His time to die for the sins of the world was coming soon, He went to Jerusalem. He rode into town on a donkey. At this time, the crowds were so impressed by His miracles that they thought Jesus had come to be their king here on earth and set them free from the rule of Rome. (Remember how Rome made them pay lots of taxes? Life under Roman rule was not very good for the Jews, and they wanted things to get better NOW.)

The people threw a parade for Jesus. They put their robes, coats, and blankets down on the road for Him to ride over (this was a sign that they were treating Him like a king). They waved palm branches and shouted, "Hosanna," which comes from a Hebrew word meaning "save" or "help." They expected Jesus to save or help them now.

Unfortunately, they didn't see the big picture that Jesus came not just to help them on this earth (because this life is so short), but He came to be their King forever, to save them from their sins and give them eternal life with Him. Over the next few days in Jerusalem, the people realized that Jesus' "kingdom is not of this world" (John 18:36), and they quickly turned their backs on Him. They praised Him on Sunday (what we celebrate as Palm Sunday because they waved the Palm branches), and then they were shouting for Jesus to die on Friday!

Have you ever had something that you wanted God to help you with or save you from *right now*? How does it feel when you don't get an answer right away or the answer isn't what you want? It may be hard to see what God is doing, but know that He is good, He is the King forever, and we can trust Him. Remember what Jesus said in John 14:1, "Do not let your hearts be troubled. Trust in God, trust also in Me."

Timeline

Say "Palm Sunday" and act like you're waving palm branches to praise Jesus. Let us remember to trust in Him even if we don't see His help right away.

Older Kids

Read John 12:12-50 in the NIrV.

JUST FOR MOM

We will continue reading in John. It is here, in Chapter 11, only about halfway through the Gospel of John, that we begin to notice a transition to Jesus' impending death. We talked earlier in this study about prophecy. God knew long before any of this took place what was going to happen. The next several chapters have a lot of prophecy: some quotes from the Old Testament that are coming true and some prophecy that Jesus reveals concerning what is about to happen to Him. Underline or somehow note all the instances of prophecy you see throughout the rest of John. Let these serve as a reminder that God knows the future and is always in control. Nothing can ever rattle Him or take Him by surprise. In the end, His plan will always persevere!

Read John 11.

What do you learn about Jesus through His relationship with Mary, Martha, and Lazarus?

Just as Lazarus died and Jesus was able to bring him back to life, soon Jesus would die and His Father would bring Him back to life.

Week 10: Holy Week

Read John 12.

What do you learn through Jesus' relationship with Mary?

What are some examples of prophecy in Chapter 12?

Reread John 12:23-29. How can these verses be a help and encouragement when you go through trials?

Read John 13.

What can we learn about how to treat others through Jesus' example?

Read John 14.

What insight do verses 1-14 give you into eternity?

Look at verses 15-31. Underline or circle all the times you see the words "love" and "obey." How are these words connected?

How will you live out your love for Jesus?

📖 *Read John 15.*

Again, underline or circle all the times you see the word "love." How was love a motivator for Jesus?

How does He want us to love Him?

How does He want us to love others?

📖 *Read John 16.*

What do you learn about the Holy Spirit?

Reflect on the power of verse 7. It is better to have the Holy Spirit within us than Jesus walking right next to us! What does that show you?

What does the Holy Spirit do for you?

Week 10: Holy Week

Read John 17.

Look at Jesus' model for prayer. He spends 6 verses praying for Himself, 15 verses praying for those closest to Him, and 7 verses praying for future believers (His Church). This can give us a guide to make sure our prayers are not only for us or even those closest to us.

How will your prayer life change because of John 17?

Look at John 17:3. Many people believe that eternal life won't begin until our life here on earth is over. But what does this verse say eternal life is? Our eternity with Jesus starts the moment we believe in Him! What aspects of eternal life have you been missing out on?

How are you going to make sure you're making the most of this life with Jesus?

KIDS DAY 2

Review the timeline up through "Palm Sunday." Remember how the people were praising Jesus as the King Who would save them on Palm Sunday? By Thursday, Judas, one of the 12 disciples, had already agreed to hand Jesus over to the Roman soldiers.

Thursday night, when Jesus and His disciples were at the meal, Jesus grabbed a bowl of water and began to wash His disciples' feet. That may seem silly to us, but back then they walked almost everywhere they went in sandals on very dirty roads that had dust, mud, animal droppings, you name it! Washing feet was the job for the lowest servant. It was dirty and yucky, kind of like if you have to clean toilets today. That didn't stop Jesus. He washed His disciples' feet to show them how much He loved them and that He was willing to serve them. He told them that just as He had served them, they now must serve one another.

Remember last week's memory verse? When He finished washing their feet, Jesus told them, "By this all people will know that you are my disciples. If you love one another." John 13:35.

Timeline

Say "feet" and rub your foot to represent Jesus washing the disciples' feet. This is a reminder that we should serve others like Jesus did, even if it's a job we don't want to do.

After Jesus had washed their feet, He began to teach them. He told them not to worry, but to trust Him. (Do you remember John 14:1?) Jesus said they shouldn't worry because He was going to Heaven to prepare a place for them, and one day He would take them there to be with Him. Thomas said, "Lord, we don't know where you are going, so how can we know the way?" (John 14:5). Jesus answered with this week's memory verse, John 14:6.

Memorize

"I am the way, the truth, and the life. No one can come to the Father except through me." -John 14:6

It is important to remember this verse because Jesus is the ONLY way to Heaven!

Older Kids

Read John 13:1-17 and John 14:1-6.

Week 10: Holy Week

KIDS DAY 3

Review the timeline up through "feet." After Jesus and His disciples finished the Last Supper on Thursday night, they went out to the Garden of Gethsemane. Jesus wanted to pray and spend some time with God the Father. When Jesus was in the garden praying, He asked His Heavenly Father to help Him. Since Jesus was human just like us, He was scared to die. He knew it wouldn't be easy. But He also knew He didn't have to do it. Jesus wanted to do whatever would make His Father happy, and He knew that in order to save you and me and the whole world from our sins, He needed to die on the cross. Jesus prayed for strength to do what God wanted Him to do.

It's important that we pray and ask God for help to be strong and brave so we can obey Him no matter what. When do you pray? Do you ask God to help you obey Him when you pray? Let's do that right now.

Timeline

Put your hands together like they're tied up and say "garden." Jesus was praying in the garden when the Roman soldiers came to arrest Him.

Older Kids

Read Matthew 26:36-46 in the NIrV.

Week 11:
Holy Week Part 2

Week 11: Holy Week Part 2

MOMS GROUP DISCUSSION

This week in the Just for Mom and Kids portions, we'll study the death of Christ, but today, we're going to focus on His resurrection.

Read John 20:11-18.

Imagine for a moment a frazzled Mary, distraught over losing her Lord and friend. Then hear in your head Jesus saying her name, "Mary."
What emotions and feelings do you think were conveyed in that one word?

Mary was the first person to see the risen Lord. Hear that clearly: Jesus appeared first to a WOMAN! Discuss Jesus' interactions with women that you can remember from our study this session. What do you think are Jesus' important messages for women? (If you want to pursue this topic more in-depth, the Bible study *Jesus and Women* by Kristi McLelland gives great insight into the culture in Jesus' day and just how radically He valued women.)

Read John 20:30-31.

Do you believe that Jesus is the Christ, the Son of God? If so, how is your life different because of that belief?

Does your family believe in Jesus? Who can we pray for right now that they would have a saving faith in Christ?

KIDS DAY 1

Review the timeline through "garden." After Jesus had finished praying, soldiers came and arrested Jesus. All through the night, Jesus was questioned by different leaders. They hit Him, whipped Him, and put a crown of thorns on His head to make fun of Him. Through all this, Jesus was silent. He didn't fight back or try to defend Himself. Early the next morning (Good Friday), the soldiers took Jesus and nailed Him to a cross to die. This was the punishment for the worst of criminals in those days. From noon until three there was darkness over the land. Then, at 3 o'clock, Jesus took His last breath. At that moment, there was a great earthquake, and even the guards at the crucifixion said, "Surely He was the Son of God!"

Timeline

Hold your arms out to the sides so you're in the shape of a cross and say, "died." Jesus willingly died on the cross for you and me so that we could live with Him again someday.

Activity

If you own a set of Resurrection Eggs, (available at most Christian bookstores), get them out and use them to talk through the events of Holy Week.

Older Kids

Read Matthew 27:27-54 in the NIrV.

JUST FOR MOM

Read John 18.

What do you notice about the character of Jesus?

How will you reflect His character?

Week 11: Holy Week Part 2

How many times did Peter deny knowing Jesus? Keep this tucked away in your mind... we'll revisit this later!

Read John 19.

Write out a prayer of love and thanksgiving to Jesus in response to what He has done for you.

Read John 20.

Don't you love that it is a woman who discovers the risen Savior first? What interactions do you remember between Jesus and Mary?

How can you tell that women are significant to Jesus?

How do you know for certain that Jesus died and rose again?

How does that impact how you live?

KIDS DAY 2

Review the timeline up through "died." After Jesus had died on the cross, they took His body down, wrapped it in cloth, and buried Him in a tomb similar to a small cave. A large rock was rolled in front to cover the entrance. Since Jesus had predicted that He would die and rise again, the Romans sealed the giant stone and placed soldiers nearby to stand guard.

Early Sunday morning (Easter) there was an earthquake. An angel came down from Heaven and rolled away the stone. The guards were so shocked they fell to the ground. Some women had come to the tomb to put spices on Jesus' body according to their custom. The angel said to them, "I know you look for Jesus, but He is not here. He has risen, just as He said." The women saw the empty tomb and they were filled with joy. They ran to tell the other disciples, and while they were on the way, Jesus met them. They worshiped Him immediately!

Timeline

Say "buried" and pretend to fall backwards with your arms over your chest. Then say "rose" and come back up with your arms out in front of you, palms up. This motion for "buried" and "rose" should remind you of our motion for "baptism." When we get baptized, it symbolizes Jesus' death and resurrection. We die to our sin and raise to new life with Jesus because of what He did for us on the cross!

Memorize

"I am the resurrection and the life. The one who believes in me will live, even though they die; and whoever lives by believing in me will never die."
-John 11:25-26

Because Jesus rose from the dead, if we believe in Him, our death on earth is not the end for us either. We will live forever with Him!

Older Kids

Read Matthew 27:62-28:10.

Week 12:
Hope for Today

MOMS GROUP DISCUSSION

Many of us know that Jesus died and rose from the dead, but what did the risen Christ do after He rose from the dead and before He ascended back up into Heaven? We know He appeared to Mary, as we studied last week. He also appeared to the disciples on two different occasions when they were gathered behind locked doors.

Read John 20:19-23.

The disciples were meeting in secret with the doors locked for fear the Jewish leaders would kill them as they had killed Jesus, so the first thing Jesus says to them is, "Peace be with you." He knew their need. Their hearts were troubled and Jesus came to meet their need for peace. Then He gives a command in verse 21- He is sending them. What does that mean?

Read verse 22. What gift does He have for them to help them in their work?

How do Jesus' command and gift apply to us today?

In John 21, Jesus appears again to the disciples as they are fishing and has a wonderful interaction with Peter. We'll look at that in the Just for Mom portion later this week.

Read 1 Corinthians 15:3-8.

Verse 8 refers to Paul's conversion where he met Jesus on the road to Damascus after Jesus' ascension into Heaven. According to this account, about how many people saw the risen Christ alive?

The most well-known instructions given by Jesus after He rose from the dead are found in Mathew 28:19-20, also known as the Great Commission (one of our memory verses for this week). But today I want us to look at another account of the Great Commission.

Week 12: Hope for Today

Read Mark 16:15-18.

What stands out to you in this passage?

How do you need to live differently in order to tap into the amazing power that Jesus has given all believers?

How has this study impacted you and your family? Who can you share it with?

KIDS DAY 1

Review the timeline through "rose." Before Jesus died, He explained to His disciples why He had to die. Of course, the main reason was to pay the price for our sins, but Jesus also needed to die and return to His Father in Heaven so He could send us His Holy Spirit. Remember how God is 3 parts in 1 God, called a Trinity? The Holy Spirit is the part of God who lives in us. Jesus told His disciples it was actually BETTER for them to have the Holy Spirit inside them than to have Jesus right next to them! That can be hard to understand, because it would be SO NEAT to spend a day with Jesus, wouldn't it? What do you think a day with Jesus would be like?

When we believe in Jesus and are baptized, the Holy Spirit comes to live in us. When we have God's Holy Spirit inside us, "the Spirit of him who raised Jesus from the dead is living in you," Romans 8:11. Imagine that: a power strong enough to raise Jesus from the dead is living in you! How does that make you feel?

The Holy Spirit helps us in many ways. Some of those ways are to guide us in truth and to convict us of sin. Have you ever felt a tug in your heart or a whisper in your mind telling you something was right or wrong? This is the Holy Spirit! We can always check and make sure it's really the Holy Spirit by asking if what we think He's telling us goes along with what we know of God in the Bible. If in doubt, ask your parents or a church leader.

Timeline

When Jesus gave the Holy Spirit to His disciples after He rose from the dead, He breathed on them and said, "Receive the Holy Spirit." Say, "Holy Spirit" as you pretend to be Jesus breathing on the disciples.

When Jesus died and rose from the dead, He overcame this world. He gave us the hope and promise that one day those who believe in Him will live with Him forever. It's through this that we can have peace, even when we face hard times. And when hard things come, remember you have God's Holy Spirit in you!

Memorize

"I have told you these things, so that in me you may have peace. In this world you will have trouble. But take heart! I have overcome the world." -John 16:33

Older Kids

Read John 14:23-27 and 16:5-15 in the NIrV.

JUST FOR MOM

Read John 21.

I love watching the full circle of Jesus' ministry. At the beginning of His ministry when He was baptized, a voice came from Heaven, and at the end of His ministry in John 12:28, a voice again comes from Heaven. Now, in Chapter 21, we see a miraculous catch of fish. Jesus first called a handful of His disciples to follow Him after providing a miraculous catch, and now, in one of the last moments the disciples will see Him on earth, He does it again. Jesus always provides. Look at the conversation between Jesus and Peter. How many times does Jesus ask Peter if he loves Him? Even though Jesus wasn't there

Week 12: Hope for Today

with Peter, He knows that Peter denied Him three times. Yet not only does Jesus forgive Peter, but He also allows Peter the chance to make things right. He gives Peter the opportunity to proclaim his love for the Lord three times.

What do you learn from Jesus' relationship with Peter throughout the book of John?

What is the biggest takeaway you have from your time reading John?

How will you live differently because of what you've learned in John and in this study as a whole?

KIDS DAY 2

Review the timeline up through "Holy Spirit." After Jesus had appeared to more than 500 people on earth, it was time for Him to return to His Father in Heaven. Jesus told the believers to go and make disciples of the whole world, baptizing them, and teaching them to obey God's commands. And He promised He would always be with them. I'm so glad Jesus is with us to give us the strength, power, courage, and wisdom to tell others about Him! How can you obey Jesus' command to teach others about Him?

Timeline

Say "ascended" (which means to go up) and lift your hands up to Heaven. Jesus ascended up into Heaven after giving the Great Commission, our next memory verse.

Memorize

"Therefore go and make disciples of all nations, baptizing them in the name of the Father and of the Son and of the Holy Spirit, and teaching them to obey everything I have commanded you. And surely I am with you always, to the very end of the age." –Matthew 28:19-20 NIV

Older Kids

Read Matthew 28:16-20 in the NIrV.

KIDS DAY 3

Review the timeline up through "ascended." Jesus is now in Heaven at God's right hand, but He won't stay there forever. God has promised that just as Jesus was lifted up into Heaven, one day He will come back down. At that time, He will make a new Heaven and a new earth and there will be no more crying, sadness, sickness, or pain for those who believe in Jesus and we will be with Him for all eternity.

What a great hope we have of what is to come! Jesus tells us we must be ready for Him to return at any time, because His coming will be a surprise. We need to be living for Him and not wasting the time He has given us on earth. It's easy to think this life is all there is, but we need to remember Jesus will return suddenly someday to make all things new. We must be ready by believing in Him and helping others to believe in Him also!

Timeline

Say "returning" and bring your hands down from the sky. We know that Jesus is returning someday to end all suffering, pain, and sadness for those who believe in Him.

Older Kids

Read Acts 1:4-11 and Revelation 21:1-4.

LEADER GUIDE
Using Guide Them to Jesus in a Moms Group Setting

12 WEEKS, 1-HOUR MEETINGS

5 minutes- Open in prayer, welcome, announcements
10 minutes- Mixer, activity, or someone shares a testimony or "Mommy tip"
5 minutes- Group review: Go over timeline motions and words and memory verses that have been covered so far
20 minutes- Group discussion- Do the "Moms Group Discussion" portion of this study in groups of ideally 6-10 people (No leader guide needed for this portion, just walk through the passages and questions provided)
20 minutes- Share prayer requests and pray in your discussion groups

12 WEEKS, 1 ½-HOUR MEETINGS

Use the schedule above, but allow 15 minutes at the beginning and end for socialization

12 WEEKS, 2-HOUR MEETINGS

20 minutes for socialization, snacks, child drop-off
5 minutes- Open in prayer, welcome, announcements
10 minutes- Mixer or activity
5 minutes- Mommy tip (can be from a different person in your group each week)
10 minutes- Personal testimony from someone in the group, ideally related to the group discussion for the day
5 minutes- Group review: Go over timeline motions and words and memory verses that have been covered so far
30 minutes- Group discussion- Do the "Moms Group Discussion" portion of this study in groups of ideally 6-10 people (No leader guide needed for this portion, just walk through the passages and questions provided)
20 minutes- Share prayer requests and pray in your discussion groups
15 minutes to socialize, clean up, pick up kids

*Alternative- you could have a guest speaker or craft for 30 minutes at some of your meetings. Those weeks, you'd omit the mixer, mommy tip, and testimony

6 WEEKS, 1-HOUR MEETINGS

5 minutes- Open in prayer, welcome, announcements
5 minutes- Mixer, activity, or someone shares a testimony or "Mommy tip"
5 minutes- Review timeline motions and memory verses
30 minutes- Do the "Moms Group Discussion" portion of this study in groups of ideally 6-10 people *You'll cover two weeks at a time in the 6-week option
15 minutes- Share prayer requests and pray in your discussion groups

6 WEEKS, 1 ½-HOUR MEETINGS

Use the schedule above, but allow 15 minutes at the beginning and end for socialization

6 WEEKS, 2-HOUR MEETINGS

Use the 12-week, 2-hour schedule, but cover two "Moms Group Discussions" each week

SPEAKER TOPIC IDEAS:

Women love the opportunity to hear in person from other women they know and trust. Pray over who from your church, your moms group, and your community could share on a particular topic. Their sharing doesn't need to be long. In fact, 20 minutes or less is usually most effective. If they can share a story from their personal experience on that topic and teach with Scripture, it will be most impactful. In the chart on the next page, I have provided passages and topics that relate to that week's group discussion. Note: the passage does not necessarily go with that topic. You can have someone base their message off either the passage OR the topic, and if they choose the topic they may be supplementing with other Scriptures.

OR

Read and teach through Mark, one chapter each week, except at the end:
Week 10: Mark 10-11
Week 11: Mark 12-13
Week 12: Mark 14-16

WEEK	SCRIPTURE
1	JOHN 1:1-18
2	MATTHEW 4:1-11
3	MARK 5:22-34
4	LUKE 5:11-26, 1 CORINTHIANS 12
5	LUKE 15
6	MATTHEW 13:24-43
7	MATTHEW 5-7
8	LUKE 11:1-18
9	JOHN 4
10	JOHN 15:1-5 OR JOHN 14-15
11	JOHN 20
12	JOHN 21

POSSIBLE TOPIC

God's plans are good and He is never surprised

Sin and temptation, knowing God's Word

Noticing "divine interruptions" in our life, finding ways to show love and minister to others even when it doesn't fit our plan

The body of believers

God searches for the lost

Living in light of eternity

Worry, heavenly treasure

Prayer

How to share your faith with others

Abiding in Christ or love and obedience

Jesus and Women (consider excerpts from "The Women of Easter" by Liz Curtis Higgs)

The Holy Spirit's role in our lives

If you have less than 12 meetings, you may have to pick which topics you feel will resonate with your group the most.

Made in the USA
Monee, IL
05 April 2025